W9-BYQ-119

THE NEED TO KNOW LIBRARY™

EVERYTHING YOU NEED TO KNOW ABOUT
BISEXUALITY

GREG BALDINO

Rosen
YA™

New York

For Teresa, burning bright in the forests of the night

Published in 2020 by The Rosen Publishing Group, Inc.
29 East 21st Street, New York, NY 10010

Library of Congress Cataloging-in-Publication Data

Names: Baldino, Greg, author.
Title: Everything you need to know about bisexuality / Greg Baldino.
Description: First Edition. | New York, NY : Rosen Publishing, 2020 | Series: The need to know library | Audience: Grades 7–12. | Includes bibliographical references and index.
Identifiers: LCCN 2018048786| ISBN 9781508187523 (library bound) | ISBN 9781508187516 (pbk.)
Subjects: LCSH: Bisexuality—Juvenile literature.
Classification: LCC HQ74 .B35 2019 | DDC 306.76/5—dc23
LC record available at https://lccn.loc.gov/2018048786

Manufactured in the United States of America

CONTENTS

INTRODUCTION

I n 2012, the Human Rights Campaign (HRC), a non-profit organization that works to advocate for people who are part of gender and sexual minorities, conducted a survey of ten thousand young people who identified as part of the LGBTQ+ community. The survey, titled "Growing Up LGBT in America," asked young people how they identified with regards to sexuality and gender and about their experiences in school, with friends, and in their families. The surveys were conducted anonymously online and were promoted both through social media and through youth centers working with LGBTQ+ youth. This method of collecting information was used to try to reach as many people as possible while giving teens the comfort of being able to speak freely about themselves. The age range of the people surveyed was thirteen to seventeen and included both middle school and high school students.

One of the questions asked on the survey was how the teens identified sexually. The available answers were heterosexual, gay, lesbian, bisexual, or queer. They could also write in another identity not listed or decline to answer the question. Approximately 40 percent of the teens surveyed identified as bisexual. A person who identifies as bisexual experiences attraction to more than one gender. Bisexual people can be any age and any gender and can have any kind of ethnic heritage. People who are bisexual live all over the world and have existed throughout history.

The LGBTQ+ community is made up of people of diverse backgrounds, experiences, and abilities, as well as different sexual and gender identities.

However, despite being so present in society, bisexual people are often the most misunderstood and underrepresented part of the LGBTQ+ community. There are many negative views of bisexuality, and accurate information about bisexual people can be difficult to find.

People who are bisexual often keep their identity secret. They may present themselves as heterosexual, attracted only to the opposite gender, or homosexual, meaning they only experience attraction to the same gender as their own. (The terms "gay" and "lesbian" are often used to refer specifically to homosexual males and females, respectively.) Because representation of bisexuality in resources and media is scarce, those who are attracted to more than one gender may feel confused and even isolated. One of the most common opinions about bisexual people is that they are "going through a phase" and that bisexuality is only a temporary identity. This viewpoint claims that bisexual people are either experimenting with homosexuality or lacking the confidence to come out "all the way."

Bisexuality is a real and valid sexual identity, one that offers a rich and complex understanding of attraction, gender, and community. There is no "right way" to be a bisexual person, and bisexuality isn't the only sexuality that experiences attraction to more than one gender.

Learning about bisexuality is important for the mental and emotional health of people who are attracted to multiple genders. For people who want to be supportive of the bisexual community, learning about their identity and their challenges helps create better allies. For anyone concerned about the struggles of the LGBTQ+ community, learning more about sexual and gender minorities is vitally important.

CHAPTER ONE

BISEXUALITY: MORE THAN EITHER/OR

Two people can be attracted to each other for many different reasons. Perhaps they have the same interests. They follow the same sports teams, watch the same TV shows, or play the same video games. If someone is nice looking, kind, funny, or a good listener, he or she can attract other people. There are different kinds of attraction; the most common is platonic attraction, which can involve close social and emotional connections. This kind of attraction can be felt toward a person's friends, a favorite teacher or librarian, or even role models and heroes like comic book creators or actors. Platonic attraction has to do with who a person is and what his or her values and behaviors are.

Sexual attraction is very different from platonic attraction. Sexual attraction is based on characteristics associated with a person's physical body: how tall he or she is, how he or she smiles or wears his or her hair, how he or she moves when he or she dances, or how he or she laughs.

People can be drawn to each other based on their shared interests, personalities, and belief systems. Platonic attraction centers around a social and emotional bond between two people.

One of the biggest factors in finding someone attractive is that person's gender, which is a set of roles, behavior, and characteristics that a society uses to recognize an individual as male or female. The genders most people are familiar with are male and female but there are more genders than just two. Some people have a nonbinary gender, meaning they may identify as having multiple genders or none at all.

BI ANY OTHER NAME

Bisexuality isn't the only identity in which people experience attraction to more than one gender. Though they are sometimes grouped together with bisexuality, each is a different identity. All of them are equal, as there's no one identity that is better or worse than the others. Pansexual people can seem very similar to bisexual people. Someone who is pansexual may describe themselves as being attracted to people of all genders or as attracted regardless of gender. Being pansexual doesn't mean that gender doesn't exist; other people's genders are an important part of their identity. But for people who identify as pansexual, whether another person's gender is similar or different to their own doesn't have any effect on their attraction to that person.

Someone who identifies as polysexual experiences sexual attraction to multiple genders, but not all of them. Some people prefer the term "pansexual" because they feel "bisexual" suggests that there are only two genders, male and female. There are some people who identify as polysexual who also identify as having a nonbinary gender and who are attracted to people on the whole range of gender expression.

Bisexuality, pansexuality, and polysexuality are different but can seem almost the same from the outside. A person who identifies as bisexual, pansexual, or polysexual can be attracted to someone who is male or female. They can be attracted to someone who is transgender, someone who identifies with a different gender than that assigned to them at birth, or who identifies as having a nonbinary gender, someone who has a gender outside the confines of male and female identity. A person is free to have whatever identity gives them the greatest sense of understanding and confidence in who they are. As a person learns more about themselves and about different identities, they may change the language they use to describe their sexual identity.

The term "queer," meaning different from the ordinary or strange, was often used in the past as a negative word to refer to homosexual people. The activist group Queer Nation reclaimed the term in the nineties, and many people in the LGBTQ+ community use "queer" as an inclusive identity to mean that someone is not heterosexual or not cisgender (a person whose gender identity matches their sex at birth) or both. Many people in the gay and lesbian community still find the term offensive, though, and its use can be controversial.

Not everyone experiences sexual attraction. Some people may identify as biromantic asexual, meaning they don't experience physical attraction to other people but can have romantic feelings for them. Not all

The word "queer," long used as a slur against LGBTQ+ people, has been reclaimed by many in the community as a way to express their gender identity and sexual orientation.

asexual people experience romantic interest, however, and some may experience romantic interest exclusively in the same gender or in a different gender. Like bisexual people, people who identify as asexual are often told that they are "going through a phase" or that their identity isn't legitimate.

COMMON MISUNDERSTANDINGS

There are a lot of misunderstandings about bisexual people and bisexuality. For people who are

A PRIDE OF THEIR OWN

Every summer, mostly in the month of June, Pride events are held around the world to celebrate LGBTQ+ people and their community. Pride events originally commemorated the 1969 Stonewall riots, during which the racially diverse, working class patrons at a gay bar in New York City fought back when the bar was raided by the police.

In 2018, the first-ever Bi Pride event was held in West Hollywood, California, on the night before the annual Bi Visibility Day. The event began with a rally followed by a parade through the city and ended with a huge party.

The idea for Bi Visibility Day originated at the 1999 International Gay and Lesbian Association World Conference. Held every year on September 23, the purpose of the event is to give much-needed attention and recognition for bisexual, pansexual, and polysexual people.

Pride events, often held in June, are celebrations of the strength and diversity of the LGBTQ+ community throughout the world.

homosexual, meaning they are attracted to their own gender, or heterosexual, meaning attracted to the opposite gender, bisexuality can seem confusing. Some believe people who identify as bisexual are experimenting or going through a phase and that they are really gay or straight. Some homosexual people think that bisexual people aren't really part of the LGBTQ+ community and are actually straight.

One of the main misunderstandings about bisexual people is the question of whether or not they have a choice about who they are. It's a misunderstanding that also applies to other identities in the LGBTQ+ community. Bisexual people can be misunderstood not only by straight people, but by members of their own community. Sometimes bisexual people are seen as being able to choose to be straight because they can experience attraction to a different gender. This can be upsetting to people who are only attracted to the same gender because when bisexual people are in a relationship that appears heterosexual, they may receive better treatment by society at large. This is called privilege and can be had by any social group that people decide is worthy of praise and acceptance.

Bisexual people may have similar experiences and feelings, but like in any community, no two bisexual people are exactly alike. For some people, being able to call themselves bisexual, pansexual, or queer helps them to understand who they are and what they feel. For other people, those are just words that mean as much about them as their zip code or phone number.

People may assume that a man and a woman in a romantic relationship are both heterosexual, but there is no way of knowing whether one or both of them identify as bisexual.

Whether a person calls themselves bisexual or polysexual or some other term is entirely up to them. A person may even refer to themselves in different ways depending on the situation. A person who identifies as polysexual may call themselves bisexual because it is a more commonly known term. Someone may feel more comfortable with people not being entirely sure of their sexuality and may call themselves queer. The only thing that matters is that people who experience attraction to more than one gender, whether sexual or romantic, are just as deserving of respect and love as anyone else.

MYTHS AND FACTS

MYTH: Bisexual people are only attracted to cisgender men and women—those who identify with the gender assigned to them at birth.

FACT: People who are bisexual can experience attraction to people of any number of genders that are either similar to or different from their own. This can include transgender men and women, people with nonbinary genders, or people who are agender.

MYTH: Bisexual people are confused about their sexuality and are really either heterosexual or homosexual.

FACT: While people of all sexualities may experience feelings of confusion as they begin to understand their attraction to other people, bisexuality is a legitimate identity that can appear in many different forms.

MYTH: A person cannot know if they are bisexual until they have been physically intimate with someone of the opposite sex.

FACT: Just as a person can know if they are heterosexual or homosexual without having been physically intimate with someone of the same or opposite gender, a person who is bisexual can feel attraction for a person regardless of whether they have experienced physical intimacy.

CHAPTER TWO

BISEXUAL ATTRACTION

There's no one definition of bisexuality. Both sexual attraction and gender identity are formed from a combination of physical, mental, and social factors; and each person's experience is unique. There has been a lot of research and many different theories about how sexual attraction and identity are formed, and there is still more to learn, but there are some basic ideas to help teens begin to understand sexuality.

A GENDER OF ONE'S OWN

To understand how bisexuality is different from heterosexuality or homosexuality, you have to understand gender and biological sex. The two topics get talked about as though they are the same thing, but while they do relate to each other, they are very different.

Biological sex begins at conception. During conception is when the chromosomes contributed by both parents combine to give the child their own chromosomal set. The most common pairs of chromosomes are XX (usually referred to as female) and XY (usually referred to as male).

The chromosomes a person gets at conception are the blueprint that organizes how their body is going to be designed. During the early stage of development, a fetus is neither anatomically male nor female, but in fact contains structures that can develop into either gender once the chromosomes become active.

To many people, the biological sex of an unborn or newborn child is very important. Parents can choose to either find out the sex of their child before birth or leave it as a surprise for when the child is delivered. After the child is born, there may be any number of ways parents

At gender reveal parties, parents and guests discover the sex of an unborn baby. However, a baby who is designated male, female, or intersex at birth may identify differently as they grow older.

celebrate, such as buying balloons and cakes declaring "IT'S A BOY!" or "IT'S A GIRL." Items ranging from diaper bags to bottle racks may be purchased in pink or blue, depending on whether the child's sex is female or male.

This is the beginning of gender for a person. Gender is the roles, behavior, and characteristics that a society uses to recognize an individual as male or female. Even today, many people judge other people's worth and ability based on their gender.

THE KINSEY SCALE

One of the most important developments in understanding bisexuality came from Dr. Alfred Kinsey. A biologist, he was a respected researcher in the field of insects. While teaching a course on marriage at Indiana University in 1938, he discovered how much his students misunderstood about sex and sexuality—and how little scientific research there was about the subject.

This led Kinsey to begin researching sexual behavior. In 1944, he conducted a series of interviews with more than five thousand men. These interviews asked a wide range of questions about their sexual experiences and ideas. The results were published in 1948 in the book *Sexual Behavior in the Human Male*, and the results were shocking to mid-century America.

One of the most important ideas from his research was a scale of sexuality, often called the Kinsey scale.

Biologist Alfred Kinsey's books on human sexuality were highly influential because his thorough research helped give this field of study legitimacy.

His research suggested that bisexuality was much more common than previously thought. Kinsey developed a scale of zero [strictly heterosexual] to six [strictly homosexual] with five different degrees of bisexuality in between. The book was controversial but also popular, becoming a best seller. Every statistic Kinsey presented was supported by thorough research and analysis. His research gave scientific evidence that homosexuality and bisexuality were much more prevalent than most people thought. His work helped lead the way for the repeal of state and federal laws that discriminated against those who were homosexual and bisexual and enabled the ongoing field of research on sexuality and gender.

THE SCIENCE BEHIND ATTRACTION

The earliest form of biological reproduction on Earth was not sexual at all; cellular organisms would simply eat, grow, and then divide into two smaller copies.

Along the way, as environmental factors made certain traits more useful than others, those microscopic organisms developed the ability to split and merge with other organisms that were different. That was the beginning of sexual reproduction.

Since then, sexuality has changed extensively, just as life-forms have. Same-sex attraction has been documented not only among humans, but among many animals as well. Scientists are still trying to understand the biology behind same-sex attraction in animals and what this can tell us about how they behave and think.

Belgian fashion model Hanne Gaby Odiele came out as a proud inter-sex person in 2017, although during her childhood, family members and doctors had advised against disclosing her condition.

Human beings are warm-blooded mammals, and the physical biology of our attraction directly originates from reproduction. The two main dynamics of biological sex are called male and female, each of which has different physical characteristics related to having children. What biological sex a person has is determined by chromosomes before they were born. Not all people are exactly male or female, though. Some people are born with physical characteristics or chromosomes that may not be entirely male or female. The term for these different conditions is intersex. It may not become apparent that a person is intersex until puberty, when sexual development begins. Some people who are intersex may have such a minor form that they may never realize any differences in their body.

Regardless of biological sex, humans and other mammals have an instinctual need for physical contact with others of the same kind. This is not strictly sexual and includes things like hugging, holding hands, pats on the back, even high fives. This kind of contact is necessary for many people to feel emotionally healthy.

Something as simple as a high five between platonic friends can create a physical connection that brings them closer together.

Human beings are drawn to physical contact, and biological sex is designed for reproduction. These two points are the foundation of sexual attraction, but they by no means dictate that a person has to have sexual contact with others if they don't want to. "No one has ever [been harmed] from not having sex," said Dr. Emily Nagasaki, author and former director of wellness education at Smith College. A person's biological sex does not determine their sexuality, even though the basic design of their chromosomes and anatomy is based on reproduction between male and female bodies.

A NEED FOR CONTACT

In 1959, psychologist Harry Harlow performed a controversial experiment in which rhesus monkeys were raised in isolation from each other. Some of the subjects were partially isolated and were able to see, smell, and hear other monkeys but had no physical contact with them. Others were kept totally apart, some for up to two years. The monkeys in both groups showed signs of emotional shock and depression from being deprived of physical contact with others. Some of the monkeys exhibited self-mutilating behavior or repetitive behavior, such as continuously circling their small cages.

Dr. Harlow's experiment was considered by many to be unethical because of the long-term harm done to the monkeys, who never fully recovered from the depravation. However, the study did present strong evidence of the importance of physical contact to mammals.

FROM SICKNESS TO HEALTH

Beginning in the early 1800s, doctors and medical researchers started to identify same-sex attraction as something that only some people were capable of experiencing. Prior to the nineteenth century, homosexuality had been seen as a sin, something opposed by religious beliefs, but also an act that a person could choose not to do. Medical doctors still considered same-sex attraction "wrong" but also as something that could be cured through treatment.

But medical doctors weren't the only ones changing their ideas about same-sex attraction. Around the world, more and more people who knew they weren't heterosexual or cisgender started to think that what they felt was real and might even be natural. The word "homosexual" first appeared in an article written in Germany in 1869 by Karl Maria Kertbeny, protesting a law that made sexual acts between men illegal. Sigmund Freud, one of the founders of early psychology, wrote in a letter to the mother of a homosexual man that same-sex attraction "... is nothing to be ashamed of, no vice, no degradation, it cannot be classified as an illness."

CHAPTER THREE

A HISTORICAL PERSPECTIVE ON BISEXUALITY

Young bisexuals may often feel as if their sexual orientation isolates them because they've been taught that attraction can only be between people of opposite genders or the same gender. In fact, not only are there people all over the world who are attracted to multiple genders, but this has been the case throughout history. Although the word "bisexual" is fairly young, bisexuality has been around for as long as there has been homosexuality—and homosexuality has been around as long as life itself.

Human history has a lot to teach us about bisexuality. In ancient Greece, it was very common for men to have both male and female partners. In some parts of Greece, having male and female partners was a standard of society—men would have wives at home, but also male partners in the military. It was believed that this helped to make the soldiers closer and helped them work better as a team. Two thousand years ago in China, bisexuality was so common that ten emperors in a row had both men and women as romantic partners. During the medieval period,

Many pieces of classical art, such as this fresco from ancient Greece, depict same-sex romantic relationships, which were not uncommon during this point in history.

when Spain was an Islamic country, one of their rulers had both a wife and several male partners. For much of the last five hundred years, in the African country known today as Benin, women could take wives as well as husbands.

SPECIAL FRIENDSHIPS AND CONTRACTUAL OBLIGATIONS

If being attracted to the same gender and to multiple genders is something that's been around for so long, why do some people think it is wrong and that being attracted to only the opposite gender is normal?

A lot of our ideas about heterosexuality being normal come from the institution of marriage. It's widely believed in the English-speaking world that marriage between a man and a woman has always happened because the two were in romantic love. This is actually a fairly recent idea, historically. Going back a few hundred years, legal marriage was something that cost a lot of money. A lot of people didn't get married because they couldn't afford it.

The origins of marriage had nothing to do with being in love. People got married to form alliances with other tribes and families and to produce children who could inherit property and help the community prosper. The idea was that if two people from two tribes or families competing for resources and territory were married and had children, those children would belong to both groups, and their families would have a reason to be peaceful and cooperative with each other. In cultures where husbands have all the power in married relationships, parents would sometimes provide money in return for a man marrying their daughter. Sometimes instead of money, a woman's property became her husband's. Often in these cultures, when the parents died, the money or property went to the son, and women couldn't have jobs, so getting their daughters married to men was the only way to make sure she would be taken care of. It was only in the last few hundred years that marriage became associated with romantic love. Some cultures still practice arranged marriages, in which the parents pick out whom their children will marry, and the bride and groom sometimes don't meet until their wedding day!

While men and women were getting married so they could have children and keep ownership of property, LGBTQ+ people were still trying to find each other for love and companionship. These relationships were sometimes called "special friendships" as a way to keep their intimacy private. Until the modern era, these people wouldn't have called themselves bisexual or gay because being physically intimate with someone of the same sex was something you did, not something you were. For the longest time, attraction to people of the same gender was seen as something you had a choice in, and so it was considered a sin or a crime and could be punished with anything from imprisonment to execution.

Before the twentieth century, life for LGBTQ+ people in North America was very different and very difficult. There were no publications about or organizations for LGBTQ+ people, no sources of information, and words like "homosexual," "transgender," and "bisexual" didn't even exist. What was expected of men and women, for most of nineteenth-century America was to live at home until marriage. Many LGBTQ+ people would keep their true sexuality or gender a secret their whole lives, never telling anyone.

As economic growth caused cities to become larger at the end of the nineteenth century and beginning of the twentieth century, they offered new opportunities for work, and more and more people moved there.

LGBTQ+ people began to find each other in the new urban environment and to form communities. They organized protest groups and published newsletters. They wrote novels and plays and recorded music that talked about what it was like to be different and how being different could be a good thing.

On June 28, 1969, police raided the Stonewall Inn, a New York City bar popular with gay and bisexual men and transgender women; many of them African American or Puerto Rican. When the police started to arrest the transwomen, one of them started fighting back. A large crowd of gay and bisexual men and lesbian and bisexual women had gathered around outside and helped attack the police. The riot lasted through the night and is

The 1969 raid on New York City's Stonewall Inn, shown here, was such a significant moment in LGBTQ+ history that in 2016 President Obama named the inn the Stonewall National Monument.

considered the beginning of the LGBTQ+ movement, as the four groups came together to further the movement and share their struggles.

PASSING: A PRIVILEGE AND A PRACTICE

Sometimes people in the LGBTQ+ community may be perceived as being heterosexual, cisgender, or both. When this happens, it's called passing, meaning they can pass themselves off as something they're not. Passing can be something a person does on purpose, where they are deliberately trying to appear as though they are not an LGBTQ+ person. They may be doing this out of fear, as they are trying to avoid being attacked for their difference. Sometimes people try to pass because they want to be seen as part of heterosexual or cisgender society, to take advantage of the safety and privilege of being in that majority.

Passing can also take place without the person involved acting intentionally. If the way that someone normally presents themselves appears heterosexual or cisgender to others, they are still able to pass, even if they have no desire to be seen as non-LGBTQ+.

Bisexual people are often accused of taking advantage of passing by some gay and lesbian people. When a bisexual person is in a relationship with someone of the opposite gender, they can both be seen as heterosexual. Similarly, when bisexual people are seen in a relationship with someone who looks like the same gender, they can both be seen as homosexual.

A WORLDWIDE BISEXUAL PANORAMA

The lives of bisexual people vary greatly around the world. Some cultures are very hostile toward people in same-sex relationships so these people have to live in secret out of fear of being attacked or imprisoned. In other parts of the world, same-sex relationships are more accepted but still not thought to be as important or real as those between men and women. In cultures like these, people in same-sex relationships may be tolerated but not allowed the right to get married. It may also not be acceptable to be out and open about being attracted to the same gender, but may be tolerated as a private relationship that is kept out of public awareness. There are cultures, though, which are much more accepting and supportive of same-sex attraction and relationships.

There are places in the world where people must hide being part of a same-sex relationship, but other cultures are more open about committment and marriage between members of the LGBTQ+ community.

The acceptance of same-sex relationships is changing constantly—and for the better in a lot of countries. As recently as 2017, homosexuality and bisexuality was made legal in the Republic of the Congo, and same-sex marriage was legally recognized in Germany, Malta, Bermuda, Finland, and other countries. That same year, same-sex couples gained the right to adopt children in Nepal, Paraguay, and Mongolia. It became illegal to discriminate against someone because of their sexual orientation in Peru, Sri Lanka, the Mexican state of Nuevo León, and the Canadian provinces of Quebec and Newfoundland. In the United States, a major victory for bisexual and homosexual people took place in 2015, when the Supreme Court struck down all state bans on same-sex marriage. All around the world, bisexual people are helping to shape a better, safer world for the LGBTQ+ community.

CHAPTER FOUR

DEALING WITH PREJUDICE

Bisexual people may have questions and concerns as they explore their identity and their attraction to more than one gender. They may want to talk about these complicated feelings with someone who can offer guidance and support.

Not everyone wants to listen, though. Some people can behave negatively toward bisexual people or say unkind things about them. This is called biphobia, a fear or hatred of bisexual people.

Biphobia can take many different forms and can come from many different people or communities. The negativity can come from heterosexual people who don't like homosexual people and include bisexual people in that dislike. This can include religious groups that consider bisexual and homosexual people sinful for being intimate with the same gender. It can also include businesses and political institutions that deny services and rights to people in same-gender relationships.

Sometimes biphobia isn't as obvious as being openly mean to someone or to the bisexual community as a whole. Other forms of biphobia can include excluding

Although the right of LGBTQ+ people to marry has been established in the United States, there are still those who protest these unions, at times using religion as the basis for their prejudice.

bisexual people from being considered a legitimate identity, claiming that being bisexual is "just a phase," or believing that those who refer to themselves as bisexual are just trying to appear hip and get attention.

One of the difficulties for bisexual people with addressing biphobia from some in the heterosexual community is that often the bias becomes apparent only when they are in a same-sex relationship. Bisexual people who are in a different-gender relationship or single may be considered straight and given the privilege that goes along with appearing heterosexual. For a lot of bisexual people, getting this consideration doesn't make up for knowing that they are attracted to other genders and would be viewed very differently by the same people who are warm and welcoming to the person they view as straight.

On the other hand, some gay and lesbian people view bisexual people as taking advantage of straight privilege, meaning they benefit in society because they can appear to be heterosexual. A frequent prejudice is that because bisexual people are attracted to more than one gender, they have the option to choose to be in a same-sex or a different-sex relationship and may choose to be with someone of a different gender to take advantage of being seen as straight. Another belief that some people have held is that people who are attracted to more than one gender are unfaithful in relationships because they are always wanting to be romantically or sexually involved with other people of a different gender from their partner. Being bisexual doesn't mean that a person cannot be faithful to one person. But some may be in a relationship in which both partners agree that they can be involved with other people as well; they may even have a partner they are both dating. There's no correct type of relationship for everyone.

One of the things about the word "bisexual" that can create misunderstanding is the prefix "bi," which is used to refer to a pair of things, like the two wheels on a bicycle. Many people take the "bi" to mean that bisexual people are only attracted to two genders, male and female. Some people who are transgender say this is transphobic and that bisexual people are only attracted to cisgender people and don't consider transgender men and women to be legitimate partners. Other transgender people think bisexual people don't recognize nonbinary people. This assumption is another form of biphobia and ignores bisexual people who are also transgender. Being bisexual doesn't make a person transphobic any more than being transgender makes a person biphobic.

In addition to biphobia, something else that affects bisexual people is when their sexuality is not recognized or is treated as if it didn't exist. This is known as bi erasure and can contribute to people not realizing their own identity. Erasure of bisexuality can appear in things such as scientific research or surveys asking people for their demographic information. A bisexual person presented with a question asking whether they are homosexual or heterosexual cannot answer truthfully, and other questions related to their sexuality may also be answered incorrectly.

Bi erasure can make it more difficult to identify bisexual people throughout history. Sometimes this erasure is unintentional; in historical times when attraction to multiple genders was more commonly accepted, there were not words to describe such an identity. This attraction would not have been seen as out of the ordinary, so people may have not mentioned it in memoirs or personal letters.

Historians may contribute to bi erasure without intending to do so. If attraction to the same gender was viewed as wrong and criminal, people would keep it secret. Written records would leave out information about a person's sexuality to protect them. In the last century, especially as media became more accessible and widespread, family members of deceased bisexual and homosexual people often tried to cover up their loved one's true identity. In addition to people's same-sex attraction being hidden, for many years,

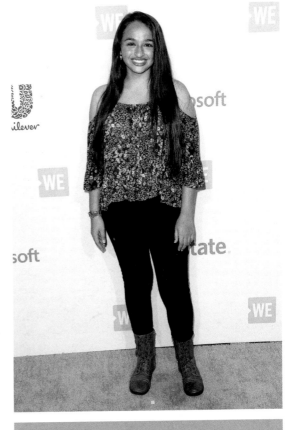

Jazz Jennings is an LGBTQ+ activist who has documented her journey as a transgender teen on television and in books.

In a 2016 interview with the Huffington Post bisexual actress Sara Ramirez stated, "You're good enough just the way you are. Your voice matters, your feelings matter and you belong here."

homosexual men and women have maintained relationships with people of the opposite gender to help conceal their identity. So even if a historical figure is revealed to have experienced attraction to a person of the same gender or even maintained a relationship with them, it can be difficult to determine what their true sexual identity was.

How the media portrays bisexual people in television and movies can have a great impact. Seeing characters who are attracted to more than one gender helps audiences recognize and understand people who are bisexual, pansexual, or other identities that they may not recognize in their everyday lives. It is particularly important for bisexual teens to see their lives reflected in creative works so they feel supported, which is essential for their development.

However, sometimes LGBTQ+ representation on television can be harmful. Characters who are recognized as bisexual can be made into a negative stereotype, especially in stories centered on gay or lesbian characters who talk about bisexual characters as traitors or as deceitful. Other times, characters are presented as if they are members of the LGBTQ+ community but are never shown in a romantic relationship with someone of the same gender.

When a work of entertainment suggests that a character is homosexual or bisexual but never actually affirms the character's sexuality or identity, it's called queer baiting. Writers and producers of movies, TV shows, and even comic books use this tactic to draw in viewers and readers who are LGBTQ+ or who are supportive allies but then never actually give representation to different sexual or gender identities. Queer baiting may involve having a character appear to be gay as some sort of running joke. In interviews and on social media, the creators or performers involved may openly deny a character being attracted to the same or multiple genders. For bisexual people, this can be extremely upsetting; not only are they denied representation, but they may also feel that their identity is not even allowed to exist in fiction.

EXITING THE CLOSET

One of the most common experiences to every identity in the LGBTQ+ community is coming out of the closet. The phrase dates back to the 1960s and means that a person is no longer hiding their true self and is now living their life as an openly homosexual, bisexual, or transgender person.

Heterosexual and cisgender people never have to come out about their sexual or gender identity. For them, the closet doesn't exist. Members of the LGBTQ+ community have to make a decision at some point in their lives about whether to come out or not. Some people choose to stay in the closet for a long time, and some make the decision to never come out.

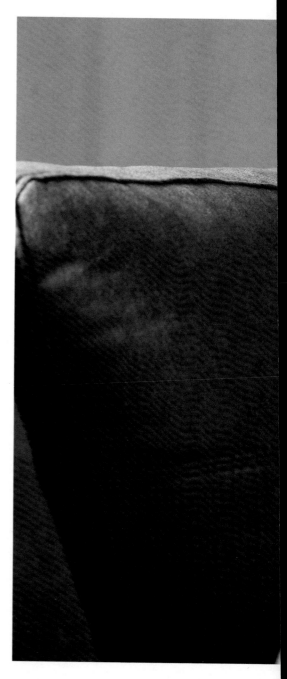

Biphobia can lead to feelings of isolation and sadness, but bisexual people can have satisfying friendships and romantic relationships that contribute to both their physical and emotional well-being.

There are many different reasons why a person may choose to stay in the closet. They may be afraid of abuse from their family or bullying at school. Their country may have laws against same-sex relationships or being transgender. Some may have a partner who they fear may be hurt if they came out. Many bisexual people stay in the closet because they're unsure what their sexuality really is—whether they are bisexual or homosexual, pansexual, or something else entirely. Many religious institutions have rules about sexual identity; people who work for a religious organization or attend a private religious school may stay in the closet to avoid losing their job or being expelled from school.

There can be consequences, however, to staying in the closet about one's sexual or gender identity. The longer a person stays in the closet, the more emotionally exhausting it may become. Staying closeted means pretending to be something you're not every day of your life. That choice can lead to closing oneself off from a supportive community, which can be isolating. Being in the closet means telling secrets and lies to those closest to you and never knowing how they may feel about the real you. People who stay in the closet have to deny who they really are and may even internalize biphobic ideas to justify keeping the secret. Someone in the closet may even be hostile to other bisexual people to keep from being found out.

Remaining closeted can take so much energy and effort that some might feel that they have to keep pretending to justify what they are putting themselves

BEING BISEXUAL

There is no one right way to express your bisexual identity. The following artists share their thoughts on being part of the bisexual community:

When I was a wee baby bisexual, I combed through every book and TV show and movie for validation that I deserved love and sex and friends and everything. I was 12 and I didn't have much luck. But then online, for the first time in my life, I started to read about happy queers. Bisexuality was real. Queer people had fulfilling and exciting lives. I could read about a potential positive, even normal outcome for my life. This idea kept me living it.
Gaby Dunn, author and comedienne

I've spent my life uncomfortable with all the relevant labels. To describe myself as straight feels deceptive. It's probably most appropriate to say I'm somewhere on the bisexual spectrum. The only reason I'm saying it to you is that it basically feels like an elephant in the room.
Kieron Gillen, comic book writer

To be bi is a continuous series of coming out moments—first to yourself, maybe next it's to your sister. Then maybe you come out to your friends. And then you'll brace yourself and come out again and again and again to every person you'll ever date. When does it end? When do people start to grasp that this is your truth?
Stephanie Beatriz, actress

When coming to terms with your sexual orientation or gender identity, it can be helpful to have a trusted adult to serve as a sounding board and informational resource.

concern for many people regarding coming out is the reactions from other people. For younger bisexual people, they may worry about being bullied or being treated differently. A common fear for people coming out is losing friendships or being rejected by family. Older people who come out as being attracted to more than one gender may still worry about how they will be treated but can have other considerations, such as the obligations of marriage and children, or how others may react if they have been living openly as a homosexual person.

There are many different ways for a person to come out about their identity. What matters most is that they are able to choose a method that will be comfortable for them. This may involve sitting down one on one with a trusted person for a private talk. Other people may prefer to have the discussion over the phone or in an online chat. Someone else might choose to write a letter so that they can take their time and communicate all their thoughts and feelings about the subject into a single statement.

People who are told that their loved one is bisexual may need time to adjust to the news, even if they are supportive. They may have questions and the friend or family member who is coming out to them may not have all the answers. This doesn't mean that they are not really bisexual. People grow and learn about themselves and their sexuality throughout their lives.

It may feel more comfortable for teens to come out for the first time to someone who isn't a part of their everyday life. For young people, this could be someone such as a school counselor, a youth services librarian, or a friend from another school or summer camp whom they don't see on a regular basis. Many LGBTQ+ organizations also have meetings and resources for young people.

Creating a base of support and understanding helps make coming out easier. It can also help people who may be struggling with their own identity to see others living openly and to see that being bisexual is something that doesn't have to be hidden. Living openly and honestly can bring its own peace of mind.

BISEXUAL ACTIVISM

For bisexual people and their allies, biphobia in its many forms creates discomfort and makes it hard to be out and open about their sexuality. Coming from heterosexual people, biphobia can indicate a lack of tolerance and disregard for the safety of other people in the LGBTQ+ community as well. Within the LGBTQ+ community, this mind-set creates a culture of division and exclusion. But biphobia can be challenged and overcome to create safer spaces and a more inclusive community.

The fear and dislike of bisexual people can appear in many different situations and from many different people. One significant difference is whether the instance or action of biphobia comes from intention, in which a person or organization is deliberately attacking or excluding bisexual people, or ignorance, in which someone may not even realize that their actions or words are causing harm.

The following are some ways to support the bisexual community from biphobia:

- **Call out negative language.** When someone makes a mean remark or joke about bisexual people, letting them know that what they are saying is not acceptable and makes people uncomfortable may help to stop it from happening more in the future.
- **Ask for bisexual inclusion.** Events and organizations may mention gay and lesbian people but

leave out other identities in the LGBTQ+ community. Asking for bisexual people to be included and named alongside gay and lesbian people helps to raise awareness.

- **Learn more.** Understanding is a powerful tool for overcoming prejudice and hatred. Listening to bisexual people talk about their experiences and reading about bisexuality helps create an environment of tolerance and makes it easier to recognize and call out biphobia when it inevitably appears.

THE PRIDE FLAGS

You may have seen the rainbow flag with horizontal stripes as a symbol for the LGBTQ+ community on display in neighborhoods and businesses, particularly during Pride festivals. The rainbow flag was created by Gilbert Baker in 1977. He was asked to design a symbol of pride for the gay community of San Francisco, California, by Harvey Milk, the first openly homosexual person elected to a major government position. The flag has gone through a few changes since the original version; moving from eight colored stripes to six: red for life, orange for healing, yellow for sunlight, green for nature, blue for harmony, and purple for spirit.

There are also pride flags for other LGBTQ+ identities. The bisexual pride flag was designed by Michael

(continued on the next page)

(continued from the previous page)

Page in 1998 and has three left to right stripes in pink, lavender, and blue. The pink stripe symbolizes same-sex attraction, the blue stripe opposite-sex attraction, and the lavender stripe a blending of the two to represent bisexual attraction. There is also a flag for pansexual pride, with side-to-side stripes in pink (for those who identify with the female gender spectrum, blue (for those who identify with the male gender spectrum), and yellow (for those who identify as nonbinary).

The pink, lavender, and blue stripes of the bisexual pride flag can be seen at many LGBTQ+ events and other venues where members of the community gather for friendship and support.

CREATING COMMUNITY

Bisexual people are a part of the larger LGBTQ+ community, but being in contact with people who share the same struggles and experiences can be helpful and healing. Creating a community for people who experience attraction to more than one gender can seem like a big task to take on, but it doesn't have to be.

There's no set number for how many people it takes to form a support group. It can be as small as two people who can be open with each other and offer guidance. It can be as official as a school organization with regular meetings or as casual as a group of friends getting together to talk about their fears, frustrations, and triumphs. A group can meet in person at a regular time and place or stay in contact digitally, through text messages, chat groups, and blogs.

What a bisexual community group does depends on the needs of its members. At the very least, it is a social space where people can feel safe being open about their identities. But sexuality isn't the only thing a bisexual community can provide its members. The people in such a community may be struggling with different issues including racial discrimination, disability and medical needs, poverty, abuse, and mental health concerns. Even if those issues may not be shared by everyone in the group, they can still support one another and foster pride, community, and a true sense of connection.

10 GREAT QUESTIONS TO ASK AN LGBTQ+ ADVOCATE

1. How can I be certain that I am bisexual?
2. Should I tell my partner if I think I might be bisexual?
3. Is coming out always the right choice?
4. Can a transgender person also be bisexual?
5. Is bisexuality transphobic?
6. Why is bisexual visibility important?
7. How do different religions view bisexuality?
8. Where can I turn for help in dealing with issues related to my sexual orientation?
9. Who are some notable bisexual people in our society?
10. How can I advocate for issues important to the bisexual community?

GLOSSARY

agender Not identifying as any particular
gender; genderless.

bi erasure A lack of recognition or acknowledgment of
the bisexual community.

biological sex Physical characteristics related to biological reproduction.

biphobia A fear or hatred of bisexual people
and bisexuality.

bisexual To be attracted to people whose gender is
similar to or different from one's own.

cisgender Identifying with the gender identity one was
assigned at birth, usually male or female.

gender The roles, behavior, and characteristics that
a society uses to recognize an individual as male
or female.

heterosexual A person who is attracted to someone of
the opposite sex.

homosexual A person who is attracted to someone of
the same sex or gender.

internalize To have an idea become ingrained in a
person's core set of beliefs.

intersex Having sexual characteristics or chromosomes that do not conform to strict definitions of
male or female.

Kinsey scale A numerical scale used to determine
a person's sexual orientation at a given time in
one's life.

pansexual Attracted to people regardless of their
gender identity or biological sex.

53

passing Seeming to belong to a particular privileged group based on outward appearances.

platonic attraction Nonsexual attraction that can involve close social and emotional connections.

polysexual Attracted to multiple genders, but not all of them.

queer A term used by some people to mean not heterosexual or not cisgender. Sometimes used as an insult.

sexual attraction A physiological response felt by someone who desires sexual contact with another person.

sexual orientation A person's pattern of sexual attraction.

transgender Identifying with a gender identity different from the one assigned at birth.

FOR MORE INFORMATION

The Center
208 W. 13th Street
New York, NY 10011
(212) 620-7310
Website: https://gaycenter.org
Facebook and Instagram: @lgbtcenternyc
Twitter: @LGBTCenterNYC
The Lesbian, Gay, Bisexual, and Transgender Community Center is located in New York City's Greenwich Village and features community spaces, a bookstore, and a coffee shop.

It Gets Better
Website: https://itgetsbetter.org
YouTube: It Gets Better Project
Founded by the writer Dan Savage, It Gets Better is a social media project to support LGBT youth with videos encouraging them and letting them know that however difficult their situation, a happy, healthy life is possible for LGBT-identifying people.

Jeunes Queer Youth
2075 Rue Plessis
Montréal QC H2L 2Y4
Canada
(514) 826-8806
Website: https://jeunesqueeryouth.org
Facebook: @jeunesqueeryouth
This program is run by five Montreal community

organizations: AIDS Community Care Montreal, Action Santé Travesti(e)s et Transsexuel(le)s du Québec, the Montreal Coalition of LGBT Youth Groups, Project 10, and Rézo. The program provides LGBT youth with the funds and resources to produce their own sexual education initiatives.

LGBT Youth Line
PO Box 73118, Wood Street PO
Toronto, ON M4Y 2W5
Canada
(800) 268-9688
Website: http://www.youthline.ca
This youth-led organization affirms and supports the experiences of youth across the Canadian province of Ontario. It provides anonymous peer support and resources.

Outfront Kalamazoo
340 S. Rose Street
Kalamazoo, MI 49007
(269) 349-4234
Website: http://outfrontkzoo.org
Facebook: @OutFrontKzoo
Instagram: @outfront_kzoo
Twitter: @OUTFRONT_KZOO
Located in southwest Michigan, Outfront provides services and resources to youth and adults from the greater Kalamazoo region. They regularly feature the artwork of local LGBT artists and host an annual Pride celebration.

Scarleteen
Website: http://www.scarleteen.com
Facebook and Twitter: @Scarleteen
Instagram: @scarleteenorg
This website for teens provides information and
    resources on sexual health, sexuality, and gender
    identity. It also hosts forums for the discussion of
    different sexuality-related topics.

The Trevor Project
PO Box 69232
West Hollywood, CA 90069
(866) 488-7386
Email: info@thetrevorproject.org
Website: http://thetrevorproject.org
Facebook: @TheTrevorProject
Twitter: @TrevorProject
YouTube: The Trevor Project
Founded in 1998, the Trevor Project mission is to
    provide crisis intervention and suicide prevention
    services for lesbian, gay, bisexual, transgender, and
    asexual youth.

FOR FURTHER READING

Baldino, Greg. *The Early History of the Gay Rights Movement.* New York, NY: Rosen Publishing, 2019.

Dunn, Gaby, and Allison Raskin. *I Hate Everyone But You: A Novel.* New York, NY: Wednesday Books, 2017.

Langford, Jo. *The Pride Guide: A Guide to Sexual and Social Health for LGBTQ Youth.* London, UK: Rowman & Littlefield, 2018.

Lee, Mackenzie. *The Gentlemen's Guide to Vice and Virtue.* New York, NY: Katherine Tegen Books, 2017.

Levithan, David. *The Full Spectrum: A New Generation of Writing About Gay, Lesbian, Bisexual, Transgender, Questioning, and Other Identities.* New York, NY: Knopf Books, 2008.

Mardell, Ashely. *The ABCs of LGBT.* Miami, FL: Mango Media, 2016.

Moon, Sarah, and James Lecesne. *The Letter Q: Queer Writers' Notes to Their Younger Selves.* New York, NY: Arthur A. Levine Books, 2012.

Prager, Sarah. *Queer There and Everywhere.* New York, NY: Harper Collins, 2017.

Savage, Dan, and Terry Miller. *It Gets Better: Coming Out, Overcoming Bullying, and Creating a Life Worth Living.* New York, NY: Penguin Books, 2011.

Stevenson, Robin. *Pride: Celebrating Diversity & Community.* Victoria, British Columbia: Orca Books, 2016.

Wang, Jen. *The Prince and the Dressmaker.* New York, NY: First Second Books, 2018.

BIBLIOGRAPHY

Beatriz, Stephanie. "Stephanie Beatriz Is Bi and Proud as Hell." GQ, June 21, 2018. https://www.gq.com /story/stephanie-beatriz-is-bi-and-proud-as-hell.

Belge, Kathy, and Mark Bieske. *Queer: The Ultimate LGBT Guide for Teens.* San Francisco, CA: Zest Books, 2011.

Cover, Rob. *Queer Youth Suicide, Culture and Identity.* Surrey, UK: Ashgate Publishing, 2012.

Deschamps, David, and Bennett Singer. *LGBTQ Stats.* New York, NY: The New Press, 2017.

Dunn, Gaby. "The Bisexual Character in My YA Novel Isn't Perfect—Which Is Perfect." Autostraddle, September 18, 2017. http://www.autostraddle.com /writing-a-bisexual-character-gaby-dunn-393649.

Eisner, Shiri. *Bi: Notes for a Bisexual Revolution.* Berkeley, CA: Seal Press, 2013.

Fish, Linda Stone. *Nurturing Queer Youth: Family Therapy Transformed.* New York, NY: W. W. Norton, 2005.

Freud, Sigmund. Sigmund Freud to Mrs. [redacted], April 9, 1935. The Kinsey Institute, Bloomington, IN. Manuscript.

Gillen, Kieron. "Writer Notes: Phonogram: The Immaterial Girl." Another Way to Breathe, April 6, 2016. http:// kierongillen.tumblr.com/post/142320486617 /writer-notes-phonogram-the-immaterial-girl.

Harlow, Harry F., et al. "Total Social Isolation in Monkeys." *Proceedings of the National Academy of Sciences of the United States of America* 54, no. 1 (1965): 90–97.

Kertbeny, Karl Maria. "Paragraph 143 of the Prussian Penal Code of 14 April 1851 and Its Reaffirmation as Paragraph 152 in the Proposed Penal Code for the North German Confederation. An Open and Professional Correspondence to His Excellency Dr. Leonhardt, Royal Prussian Minister of Justice." *Jahrbuch fuer sexuelle Zwischenstufen* 7, no. 1 (1905): i-iv, 1-66.

Langford, Jo. *The Pride Guide: A Guide to Sexual and Social Health for LGBTQ Youth.* London, UK: Rowman & Littlefield, 2018.

Madison, Amber. *Talking Sex with Your Kids.* Avon, MA: Adams Media, 2010.

Mardell, Ashley. *The ABCs of LGBT.* Miami, FL: Mango Media, 2016.

Newton, David E. *LGBT Youth Issues Today.* Santa Barbara, CA: ABC-CLIO, 2014.

Prager, Sarah. *Queer There and Everywhere.* New York, NY: Harper Collins, 2017.

Seba, Jamie A. *Gay Issues and Politics: Marriage, the Military, and Work Place Discrimination.* Philadelphia, PA: Mason Crest, 2011.

Seba, Jamie A. *Gays and Mental Health: Fighting Depression, Saying No to Suicide.* Philadelphia, PA: Mason Crest, 2011.

INDEX

ABOUT THE AUTHOR

Greg Baldino holds a bachelor of arts in fiction writing from Columbia College Chicago, where he studied radical literature and twentieth-century cultural history. Since 2007, he has written for many different publications as a journalist and essayist on topics such as alternative fashion, folk music, Italian cooking, criminal psychology, antifascist activism, digital media, architectural theory, comics and graphic novels, gender politics, environmental science, and the performing arts. He lives in Michigan surrounded by tall trees and fine coffee.

PHOTO CREDITS